DOLLARS AND SENSE

A TEEN'S GUIDE TO CREDIT

MANDY OGLETHORPE

Copyright © 2024 Mandy Oglethorpe

All rights reserved. This publication, or any part thereof, may not be reproduced in any form or by any means, including electronic, photographic, or mechanical, or by any sound recording system or by any device for storage and retrieval of information without the written permission of the copyright owner.

Contents

Chapter 1: Understanding Credit 5

    Introduction to Credit: What Is Credit, and Why Is It Important? 5

    Credit Scores and Reports 6

    Types of Credit 9

    Impact of Credit on Financial Health 12

Chapter 2: Building Credit Responsibly 15

    Establishing Credit as a Teenager 15

    Tips for Building a Positive Credit History 17

    Understanding the Importance of On-Time Payments .. 20

    How to Manage Credit Responsibly 22

Chapter 3: Managing Credit Cards 25

    Choosing the Right Credit Card for Your Needs 25

    Understanding Credit Card Terms and Conditions 27

    Using Credit Cards Wisely 30

    Avoiding Common Credit Card Pitfalls 32

Chapter 4: Using Credit for Major Purchases 35

    Understanding Loans and Financing Options 35

    Tips for Responsibly Using Credit for Big Purchases 37

    How to Compare Loan Offers and Interest Rates 40

    Avoiding Debt Traps When Making Major Purchases .. 43

Chapter 5: Protecting Your Credit 46

    Importance of Monitoring Your Credit Report: 46

    How to Detect and Prevent Identity Theft 48

    Steps to Take If You Become a Victim of Fraud 51

    Tips for Safeguarding Your Personal Information 53

Chapter 6: Credit for the Future 57

    Planning for the Future with Credit in Mind 57

    Understanding the Long-Term Impact of Credit Decisions 59

    Setting Financial Goals and Using Credit Wisely to Achieve Them 61

    Tips for Maintaining Good Credit Throughout Your Life 63

Conclusion 66

Chapter 1:
Understanding Credit

Introduction to Credit: What Is Credit, and Why Is It Important?

Credit is a financial tool that allows individuals to borrow money or access goods and services with the promise to repay the amount borrowed at a later date. It is essentially an agreement between a borrower and a lender, where the borrower receives funds or goods upfront and agrees to pay back the amount borrowed, usually with interest, over a specified period of time.

Credit plays a crucial role in modern society, as it enables individuals to make large purchases, such as buying a car or a home, that they may not be able to afford outright. It also provides a convenient way to cover unexpected expenses or emergencies without having to deplete savings. By using credit responsibly, individuals can build a positive credit history, which can help them qualify for better interest rates on loans, secure rental housing, and even land a job in some industries.

Understanding how credit works and how to manage it effectively is essential for financial success. It is important for teens to learn about the different types of credit available, such as credit cards, loans, and mortgages, as well as the potential risks and benefits associated with each. By learning how to use credit responsibly, teens can avoid falling into debt and build a solid foundation for their financial future.

Credit Scores and Reports

Understanding credit scores and reports is essential for teenagers as they begin to navigate the world of personal finance. In this section, we will delve into what credit scores and reports are, why they matter, and how they can impact financial decisions now and in the future.

What are Credit Scores and Reports?

A credit score is a three-digit number that represents an individual's creditworthiness. It is a numerical reflection of a person's credit history and how likely they are to repay borrowed money. Credit scores typically range from 300 to 850, with higher scores indicating better creditworthiness.

On the other hand, a credit report is a detailed record of an individual's credit history. It includes information such as credit accounts, payment history, outstanding balances, and any negative marks like late payments or accounts in collections. Credit reports are maintained by credit bureaus and are used to calculate credit scores.

Why Do Credit Scores and Reports Matter?

Credit scores and reports play a crucial role in a teenager's financial life. Lenders, landlords, insurance companies, and even potential employers may use this information to assess an individual's financial responsibility. A good credit score can lead to lower interest rates on loans, better rental opportunities, and cheaper insurance premiums.

By understanding credit scores and reports, teens can take steps to build and maintain a positive credit history, setting themselves up for financial success in the future. On the flip side, neglecting credit can lead to difficulties in obtaining loans, higher interest rates, and limited financial opportunities.

How Can Teens Improve Their Credit Scores?

There are several ways teenagers can improve their credit scores and build a positive credit history. The following are some helpful tips:

1. **Pay bills on time:** Timely payments are one of the most critical factors in determining credit scores. Encourage teens to pay bills, such as credit card bills, student loans, and utilities, on time every month.
2. **Use credit wisely:** Teens should be cautious about taking on too much debt. Keeping credit card balances low and avoiding maxing out credit lines can positively impact credit scores.
3. **Monitor credit reports:** Teens should regularly review their credit reports to check for errors or signs of identity theft. Correcting any inaccuracies can help maintain a healthy credit profile.
4. **Establish credit responsibly:** Teens can start building credit by becoming an authorized user on a parent's credit card or applying for a secured credit card. These responsible credit habits can set a strong foundation for their financial future.

In conclusion, understanding credit scores and reports is

crucial for teenagers as they step into the world of credit and finance. By taking proactive steps to build and maintain good credit, teens can set themselves up for a financially secure future.

Types of Credit

Credit is a financial tool that allows individuals to borrow money or make purchases on the promise of repaying the borrowed amount in the future. There are various types of credit available to consumers, each with its own features and considerations. In this section, we will discuss two common types of credit: credit cards and loans.

1. Credit Cards:

Credit cards are a popular form of credit that allows cardholders to make purchases up to a certain credit limit set by the card issuer. Here are some key points to understand about credit cards:

- **Revolving Credit:** Credit cards provide a revolving line of credit, which means that cardholders can borrow up to their credit limit, repay the borrowed amount, and then borrow again.

- **Interest Rates:** Credit cards typically have high interest rates, especially for unpaid balances. Paying off the full balance by the due date is important to avoid accruing interest charges.
- **Fees:** Credit cards may come with annual fees, late payment fees, cash advance fees, and other charges. Be aware of the fees associated with your credit card to avoid unnecessary expenses.
- **Rewards and Benefits:** Many credit cards offer rewards programs, cashback incentives, and other benefits for cardholders who use their cards responsibly. Consider these rewards when choosing a credit card that suits your needs.

2. Loans:

Loans are a form of credit where a borrower receives a specific amount of money from a lender and agrees to repay the borrowed amount, usually with interest, over a set period of time. Here are some common types of loans:

- **Personal Loans:** Personal loans are unsecured loans that can be used for various purposes, such as debt consolidation, home improvement, or emergency expenses. The interest rates on personal loans may vary based on the borrower's creditworthiness.

- **Student Loans:** Student loans are designed to help students pay for higher education expenses. These loans may be issued by the government or private lenders and typically offer flexible repayment options.
- **Auto Loans:** Auto loans are used to finance the purchase of a vehicle. The loan terms, interest rates, and down payment requirements may vary depending on the lender and the borrower's credit history.
- **Mortgage Loans:** Mortgage loans are long-term loans used to finance the purchase of a home. These loans typically have lower interest rates compared to other types of credit due to the collateral (the property) securing the loan.

Understanding the different types of credit available can help teens make informed decisions about borrowing money and managing their finances responsibly. It is important to borrow only what you can afford to repay, make timely payments, and build a positive credit history for future financial endeavors.

Impact of Credit on Financial Health

Credit plays a significant role in shaping individuals' financial health, especially for teenagers who are just beginning to navigate the world of personal finance. Understanding the impact of credit on financial health is crucial for making informed decisions and building a strong financial foundation for the future. The following are some important factors you should take note of:

1. Building Credit History:

Establishing a positive credit history is essential for teenagers as it sets the stage for their financial future. When used responsibly, credit can help build a strong credit score, which is a key factor in determining one's financial health. A good credit history opens doors to opportunities such as getting approved for loans, renting an apartment, or even securing a job in some cases.

2. Managing Debt:

Credit can be a double-edged sword when it comes to managing debt. While it can provide financial flexibility, excessive borrowing can lead to overwhelming debt burdens that can negatively impact financial health. Teenagers need to learn how to use credit wisely and avoid falling into the trap of debt accumulation. Understanding the importance of making timely payments and keeping debt levels in check is crucial for maintaining a healthy financial outlook.

3. Impact on Financial Goals:

Credit can either be a tool that helps teenagers achieve their financial goals or a barrier that hinders their progress. By using credit responsibly, individuals can access opportunities such as buying a car, pursuing higher education, or starting a business. However, mismanagement of credit can lead to financial setbacks and prevent teenagers from reaching their goals. Learning how to balance credit usage with financial goals is key to ensuring a positive impact on overall financial health.

4. Credit and Financial Stress:

Poor credit management can contribute to financial stress, which can have a significant impact on teenagers' overall well-being. High levels of debt, missed payments, and financial uncertainty can take a toll on mental health and relationships. Understanding the link between credit and financial stress is essential for teenagers to prioritize their financial health and make informed decisions when it comes to borrowing and spending.

In conclusion, the impact of credit on financial health is multifaceted and requires careful consideration by teenagers as they navigate the world of personal finance. By building a positive credit history, managing debt responsibly, aligning credit usage with financial goals, and minimizing financial stress, teenagers can set themselves up for a successful financial future. It is crucial for teenagers to educate themselves about the implications of credit and develop healthy financial habits early on to ensure long-term financial well-being.

Chapter 2:
Building Credit Responsibly

Establishing Credit as a Teenager

Establishing credit as a teenager is an important step toward financial independence and responsibility. While it may seem intimidating at first, building good credit early on can set you up for success in the future. Here are some key points to consider when it comes to establishing credit as a teenager:

1. Understanding the Basics:

Before you start building credit, it's crucial to understand what credit is and how it works. Credit is essentially borrowed money that you can use to make purchases, with the promise to repay the borrowed amount at a later date. Your credit history is a record of how you have managed credit in the past, and it plays a significant role in determining your credit score.

2. Start Small:

As a teenager, you may not have a long credit history or a high income, which can make it challenging to qualify for traditional credit cards or loans. However, there are several ways you can start building credit on a smaller scale. One option is to become an authorized user on a family member's credit card. This allows you to piggyback off their credit history and start building your own credit.

3. Secured Credit Cards:

Another option for teenagers looking to establish credit is to apply for a secured credit card. With a secured credit card, you'll be required to make a security deposit, which then becomes your credit limit. By using the card responsibly and making timely payments, you can start building a positive credit history.

4. Responsible Credit Card Usage:

When using a credit card to build credit, it's essential to use it responsibly. This means making purchases within your means, paying off the balance in full each month, and avoiding carrying a balance or making late payments. By demonstrating good credit habits early on, you can establish a solid foundation for your credit history.

5. Monitor Your Credit:

As you start building credit as a teenager, it's essential to monitor your credit report regularly. You can request a free copy of your credit report from each of the three major credit bureaus (Equifax, Experian, TransUnion) once a year. Reviewing your credit report can help you identify any errors or potential issues that may impact your credit score.

In conclusion, establishing credit as a teenager is a valuable step towards financial independence. By understanding the basics of credit, starting small, using credit cards responsibly, and monitoring your credit, you can lay the groundwork for a strong credit history that will serve you well in the future.

Tips for Building a Positive Credit History

Building a positive credit history is crucial to managing your finances responsibly and securing your financial future. Here are some essential tips to help teens establish and maintain a good credit history:

1. **Understand the Basics of Credit:** As discussed earlier, before you start building your credit history,

it's important to understand what credit is and how it works. Credit is essentially borrowed money that you can use to make purchases, and your credit history reflects how responsibly you manage that borrowed money.

2. **Start Early:** The earlier you start building your credit history, the better. Even if you are a teenager, you can begin by becoming an authorized user on a parent or guardian's credit card. This can help you establish a credit history and learn how credit works.

3. **Make Timely Payments:** One of the most critical factors in building a positive credit history is making your payments on time. Whether it's a credit card, student loan, or any other form of credit, be sure to pay at least the minimum amount due by the due date each month.

4. **Keep Your Credit Utilization Low:** Credit utilization refers to the percentage of your available credit that you are using. It's generally recommended to keep your credit utilization below 30% to demonstrate responsible credit management.

5. **Avoid Opening Too Many Accounts:** While having a mix of credit accounts can be beneficial for your

credit score, opening too many accounts at once can be a red flag for lenders. Be strategic about the types of credit accounts you open and only apply for credit when you truly need it.

6. **Monitor Your Credit Report:** Regularly checking your credit report can help you catch any errors or fraudulent activity that could be negatively impacting your credit score. You are entitled to a free credit report from each of the three major credit bureaus (Equifax, Experian, and TransUnion) once a year.

7. **Be Mindful of Co-Signing:** If someone asks you to co-sign a loan or credit application, think carefully before agreeing. When you co-sign, you are equally responsible for the debt, and any missed payments can harm your credit history and relationship with the primary borrower.

8. **Seek Guidance:** If you have questions about building credit or are unsure about how to manage your finances, don't hesitate to seek guidance from a trusted adult, financial advisor, or credit counselor. They can provide valuable insights and help you make informed decisions.

By following these tips and practicing responsible credit habits, teens can start building a positive credit history that will serve them well in the future. Remember, good credit opens doors to better financial opportunities, so it's worth investing the time and effort to establish and maintain healthy credit habits from a young age.

Understanding the Importance of On-Time Payments

Understanding the importance of on-time payments is crucial when it comes to managing credit effectively. Making on-time payments is a key factor in building and maintaining a good credit score, which is essential for future financial success. Here are some important factors to consider:

1. **Credit Score Impact:** When you make on-time payments towards your credit accounts, such as credit cards or loans, you demonstrate to creditors that you are a responsible borrower. This positive behavior is reported to credit bureaus and helps improve your credit score over time. On the other

hand, missing payments or paying late can have a significant negative impact on your credit score.

2. **Interest Rates:** Making on-time payments can also help you save money in the long run. When you have a good credit score due to your history of on-time payments, you are more likely to qualify for lower interest rates on loans and credit cards. This means you will pay less interest over time, ultimately saving you money.

3. **Avoiding Late Fees:** In addition to affecting your credit score, missing payments can also result in late fees and penalties. These extra charges can add up quickly and make it harder for you to pay off your debts. By making on-time payments, you can avoid these unnecessary fees and keep your overall debt under control.

4. **Financial Responsibility:** Developing a habit of making on-time payments teaches you valuable financial responsibility. It shows that you are capable of managing your finances effectively and meeting your obligations in a timely manner. This is a skill that will serve you well throughout your life as you navigate various financial decisions.

5. **Building Trust:** Consistently making on-time payments builds trust with creditors and lenders. This can lead to better future credit opportunities, such as higher credit limits or more favorable terms on loans. By demonstrating your reliability as a borrower, you can strengthen your financial standing and open doors to additional financial resources when needed.

In conclusion, understanding the importance of on-time payments is essential for any teen looking to establish a solid financial foundation. By prioritizing timely payments, you can build a positive credit history, save money on interest, avoid extra fees, and develop key financial skills that will benefit you for years to come.

How to Manage Credit Responsibly

Managing credit responsibly is a crucial skill for teens to learn as they start building their financial independence. Here are some key tips to help teens manage credit effectively:

1. **Understand the Basics:** Before using credit, teens

should understand how it works. Credit allows you to borrow money with the promise to pay it back later, often with interest. Make sure to understand the terms of any credit agreement, including interest rates, fees, and repayment schedules.

2. **Create a Budget:** Before using credit, create a budget to track your income and expenses. Knowing how much money you have coming in and going out each month will help you avoid overspending and ensure you can make your credit payments on time.

3. **Use Credit Wisely:** Only use credit for essential purchases or emergencies, not for impulse buys or luxury items. Avoid maxing out your credit cards, as high balances can negatively impact your credit score.

4. **Make Payments on Time:** One of the most important aspects of managing credit responsibly is making your payments on time. Late payments can result in fees, increased interest rates, and damage to your credit score. Set up reminders or automatic payments to ensure you never miss a due date.

5. **Pay More than the Minimum:** If you have a credit card balance, aim to pay more than the minimum

required each month. By paying more, you can reduce the amount of interest you'll pay over time and pay off your balance more quickly.

6. **Monitor Your Credit Score:** Regularly check your credit score and report to ensure there are no errors or fraudulent activity. Your credit score is a reflection of your creditworthiness and can impact your ability to borrow money in the future.

7. **Limit the Number of Credit Cards:** Having multiple credit cards can make it harder to keep track of your spending and payments. Consider starting with just one credit card and only open additional accounts if necessary.

8. **Avoid Co-signing:** While it may seem helpful to co-sign a loan for a friend or family member, it can be risky. If the primary borrower fails to make payments, you will be responsible for the debt, which could harm your credit.

By following these tips and practicing responsible credit management, teens can build a strong financial foundation and set themselves up for a successful future. It's important to remember that credit is a tool that should be used wisely and with careful consideration.

Chapter 3:
Managing Credit Cards

Choosing the Right Credit Card for Your Needs

Choosing the right credit card for your needs is a crucial decision that can have a significant impact on your financial well-being. With so many credit card options available, it's important to carefully consider your specific needs and financial habits before making a decision. Here are some key factors to consider when choosing the right credit card for you:

1. **Understand your spending habits:** Take a close look at your spending patterns to determine how you typically use your credit card. If you tend to carry a balance from month to month, look for a card with a low-interest rate. If you pay off your balance in full each month, consider a rewards credit card that offers cash back, points, or airline miles.
2. **Fees and charges:** Be aware of any annual fees, late payment fees, balance transfer fees, and foreign

transaction fees associated with the credit card. Choose a card with fees that align with your budget and spending habits.

3. **Interest rates:** Compare the APR (Annual Percentage Rate) of different credit cards to find one with a competitive interest rate. If you anticipate carrying a balance, opt for a card with a lower interest rate to minimize the amount of interest you'll pay over time.

4. **Rewards and benefits:** Consider what rewards and benefits are most important to you. Some credit cards offer cash back on purchases, travel rewards, discounts on shopping or dining, and other perks. Choose a card that provides rewards that align with your lifestyle and spending habits.

5. **Credit limit:** Determine what credit limit you need based on your monthly expenses and ability to repay the balance. A higher credit limit can be beneficial for emergencies or larger purchases, but be mindful of overspending and accruing debt beyond your means.

6. **Credit history:** Your credit score plays a significant role in the credit card approval process and the terms you may be offered. If you have a limited credit history or a lower credit score, consider applying for

a student credit card or a secured credit card to help build or improve your credit profile.

7. **Customer service and support:** Look for a credit card issuer that provides excellent customer service and support. Consider factors such as 24/7 customer service availability, online account management tools, and fraud protection services.

By carefully evaluating these factors and comparing different credit card options, you can choose a credit card that best meets your needs and helps you manage your finances responsibly. Remember to read the terms and conditions of the credit card agreement carefully and use your credit card responsibly to avoid debt and maintain a healthy financial future.

Understanding Credit Card Terms and Conditions

Credit cards can be a powerful financial tool when used responsibly, but it's crucial to understand the terms and conditions associated with them to avoid falling into debt traps. Here are some key points to consider when looking at credit card terms and conditions:

1. **Annual Percentage Rate (APR):** The APR is the interest rate you will be charged on any outstanding balance on your credit card. It's important to know the APR, as it will determine how much interest you will accrue if you carry a balance from month to month.
2. **Grace Period:** The grace period is the amount of time you have to pay your balance in full without incurring any interest charges. Typically, grace periods range from 21 to 25 days after the close of the billing cycle. Understanding your grace period is essential to avoid unnecessary interest charges.
3. **Minimum Payment:** The minimum payment is the smallest amount you must pay each month to keep your account in good standing. It's important to note that paying only the minimum will result in paying more in interest over time and can lead to long-term debt.
4. **Fees:** Credit card companies may charge various fees, such as annual fees, late payment fees, over-limit fees, and cash advance fees. Be sure to review the fee schedule in the terms and conditions to understand

what you may be charged for and how to avoid these fees.

5. **Credit Limit:** Your credit limit is the maximum amount you can borrow on your credit card. It's essential to stay within your credit limit to avoid over-limit fees and potential damage to your credit score.

6. **Rewards and Benefits:** Some credit cards offer rewards programs, cashback incentives, or other benefits for cardholders. Understanding the terms and conditions of these programs can help you maximize the benefits of your credit card usage.

7. **Penalty APR:** In case of late payments or other violations of the terms and conditions, credit card companies may impose a penalty APR, which is a higher interest rate than the regular APR. It's crucial to be aware of the circumstances that may trigger a penalty APR and how to avoid them.

8. **Credit Card Agreement:** The credit card agreement contains all the terms and conditions governing your credit card account. Be sure to read this document carefully to understand your rights and responsibilities as a cardholder.

By understanding and familiarizing yourself with the terms and conditions of your credit card, you can make informed decisions about your spending, avoid unnecessary fees and charges, and build a positive credit history. Remember to always use credit cards responsibly and within your means to maintain financial health.

Using Credit Cards Wisely

Credit cards can be a convenient tool for making purchases and building credit, but it's important to use them responsibly to avoid falling into debt. Here are some tips on how to use credit cards wisely:

1. **Pay your balance in full each month:** One of the best ways to avoid accumulating debt is to pay off your credit card balance in full each month. By doing so, you can avoid paying high interest charges and maintain a good credit score.
2. **Monitor your spending:** It's easy to overspend with a credit card since you're not using physical cash. Make sure to keep track of your purchases and stay within your budget to avoid racking up debt.

3. **Avoid impulse purchases:** Before making a purchase with your credit card, take a moment to consider if it's something you really need. Avoid impulse buys that you may regret later on.
4. **Understand your credit card terms:** Be sure to read and understand the terms and conditions of your credit card, including the interest rate, fees, and rewards program. Knowing these details can help you make informed decisions about how you use your card.
5. **Pay on time:** Late payments can result in fees and damage your credit score. Make sure to pay at least the minimum amount due by the due date to avoid these consequences.
6. **Limit the number of credit cards you have:** Having multiple credit cards can make it difficult to keep track of your spending and payments. Consider limiting the number of cards you have to only those that you need.
7. **Build your credit history:** Using your credit card responsibly can help you build a positive credit history, which is important for future financial

opportunities such as getting a loan or renting an apartment.

By following these tips and using your credit card responsibly, you can enjoy the benefits of credit cards without falling into debt. Remember to always prioritize your financial well-being and make informed decisions about your spending.

Avoiding Common Credit Card Pitfalls

Credit cards can be a useful financial tool, but they also come with risks and pitfalls that can lead to financial trouble if not managed carefully. Here are some common pitfalls to avoid when using credit cards:

1. **Overspending:** One of the biggest pitfalls of credit cards is the temptation to overspend. It can be easy to swipe your card without considering whether you can afford the purchase. To avoid this pitfall, set a budget and stick to it. Only use your credit card for purchases that fit within your budget and that you can pay off in full each month.
2. **Paying only the minimum:** When you receive your

credit card statement, you will typically have the option to pay only the minimum amount due. While this may seem like a convenient option, it can lead to a cycle of debt due to high interest rates. Always strive to pay off your full balance each month to avoid accruing interest charges.

3. **Ignoring your credit card statements:** It's important to regularly review your credit card statements to check for any errors or unauthorized charges. Ignoring your statements can lead to missed payments, late fees, and damage to your credit score. Make it a habit to review your statements each month and report any discrepancies to your credit card issuer.

4. **Falling for promotional offers:** Credit card companies often lure customers with promotional offers such as zero-interest balance transfers or cashback rewards. While these offers can be enticing, be sure to read the fine print and understand the terms and conditions. Some offers may come with hidden fees or high-interest rates once the promotional period ends.

5. **Applying for multiple credit cards:** Opening

multiple credit card accounts can make it difficult to keep track of your spending and payments, leading to potential missed payments and increased debt. Limit the number of credit cards you have and only apply for new cards when necessary.

By being aware of these common credit card pitfalls and practicing responsible credit card use, you can effectively manage your finances and build a positive credit history. Remember to use credit cards as a financial tool, not as a means to live beyond your means.

Chapter 4:
Using Credit for Major Purchases

Understanding Loans and Financing Options

Loans and financing options play a crucial role in managing your finances effectively. In this section, we will delve into the various types of loans available to teens and young adults, as well as the importance of understanding the terms and conditions associated with borrowing money.

Types of Loans:

1. **Student Loans:** Student loans are designed to help cover the costs of higher education, including tuition, books, and living expenses. It's important to research different student loan options, such as federal loans, private loans, and scholarships, and understand the terms of repayment.
2. **Personal Loans:** Personal loans can be used for a variety of purposes, such as consolidating debt, making a large purchase, or covering unexpected

expenses. Before taking out a personal loan, consider factors like interest rates, fees, and repayment terms.

3. **Auto Loans:** Auto loans are specifically for purchasing a vehicle. When exploring auto loan options, be sure to compare interest rates, loan terms, and monthly payments to find the best deal that fits your budget.

4. **Credit Cards:** While not technically a loan, credit cards allow you to borrow money up to a certain limit. It's important to use credit cards responsibly, make timely payments, and avoid carrying a balance to prevent accumulating high-interest debt.

Understanding Loan Terms:

1. **Interest Rates:** Interest rates determine how much you will pay in addition to the principal amount borrowed. Be aware of whether the interest rate is fixed or variable, as well as any potential fees associated with the loan.

2. **Repayment Terms:** Repayment terms outline how long you have to repay the loan and the frequency of payments. Understanding the repayment schedule is crucial to avoid defaulting on the loan and damaging

your credit score.

3. **Fees and Penalties:** Loans may come with various fees, such as origination fees, late payment fees, or prepayment penalties. Be sure to read the fine print and understand all potential fees associated with the loan.

4. **Credit Impact:** Taking out a loan can impact your credit score, both positively and negatively. Timely payments can help build your credit history, while missed payments can harm your credit score. Understanding the implications for your credit is essential when considering borrowing money.

In conclusion, understanding loans and financing options is essential for teens and young adults to make informed financial decisions. By researching different types of loans, comparing terms and conditions, and staying mindful of repayment obligations, you can effectively manage your finances and avoid falling into debt traps.

Tips for Responsibly Using Credit for Big Purchases

Credit can be a valuable tool when making big purchases

like a car or funding your education. However, it's important to use credit responsibly to avoid financial pitfalls. Here are some tips to help teens make informed decisions when using credit for significant expenses:

1. **Understand Your Credit Score:** Before applying for credit, it's essential to know your credit score. Lenders use this score to evaluate your creditworthiness and determine the terms of the loan. A good credit score can help you secure better interest rates and loan terms.

2. **Create a Budget:** Before taking on debt for a big purchase, create a budget to determine how much you can afford to borrow. Consider your income, expenses, and existing debt obligations to ensure you can comfortably repay the loan without straining your finances.

3. **Compare Lenders:** Don't settle for the first loan offer you receive. Shop around and compare loan terms from multiple lenders to find the best deal. Pay attention to interest rates, repayment terms, fees, and any other conditions that may apply.

4. **Borrow Only What You Need:** When using credit for a big purchase, borrow only what you need to cover

the cost. Avoid taking on excessive debt that could lead to financial stress down the road. Be realistic about what you can afford to repay based on your current financial situation.

5. **Read the Fine Print:** Carefully read the terms and conditions before signing any loan agreement. Pay attention to the interest rate, repayment schedule, fees, and any penalties for late payments. Make sure you understand all the terms of the loan before committing to it.

6. **Make Timely Payments:** One of the most important factors that affect your credit score is your payment history. Always make your loan payments on time to avoid late fees and negative marks on your credit report. Set up automatic payments or reminders to ensure you don't miss any deadlines.

7. **Avoid Maxing Out Your Credit:** Try to keep your credit utilization ratio low by not maxing out your credit cards or loans. Using too much of your available credit can hurt your credit score and make it harder to borrow in the future. Aim to keep your credit utilization below 30% of your total credit limit.

8. **Plan for Unexpected Expenses:** When taking on debt

for a big purchase, consider setting aside an emergency fund to cover unexpected expenses or financial setbacks. Having a buffer can help you avoid relying on credit cards or loans to cover unforeseen costs.

By following these tips and using credit responsibly, teens can make informed decisions when financing big purchases like a car or education. Remember that credit is a financial tool that, when used wisely, can help you achieve your goals and build a positive credit history for the future.

How to Compare Loan Offers and Interest Rates

When looking at loan offers and interest rates, it's important to understand the key factors that can affect the overall cost of borrowing money. Here are some steps to help you effectively compare loan offers and interest rates:

1. **Identify the Type of Loan You Need:** Before comparing loan offers, determine the type of loan you need based on your financial goals and circumstances. Common types of loans include personal loans, auto loans, student loans, and

mortgages.

2. **Check Your Credit Score:** Lenders use your credit score to determine the interest rate they offer you. A higher credit score usually results in a lower interest rate, saving you money in the long run. Before comparing loan offers, check your credit score and take steps to improve it if necessary.

3. **Understand the Annual Percentage Rate (APR):** The APR is a key factor in comparing loan offers as it represents the total cost of borrowing, including both the interest rate and any additional fees. Always compare the APR of different loan offers to get a clear picture of the total cost.

4. **Consider the Loan Term:** The loan term refers to the length of time you have to repay the loan. While a longer loan term may result in lower monthly payments, it can also mean paying more in interest over the life of the loan. Consider the trade-off between monthly payments and total interest costs when comparing loan offers.

5. **Compare Interest Rates:** Interest rates can vary significantly between lenders, so it's essential to compare rates to get the best deal. Keep in mind that

fixed interest rates remain the same throughout the loan term, while variable interest rates can fluctuate based on market conditions.

6. **Look for Prepayment Penalties:** Some loans come with prepayment penalties, which charge you a fee for paying off the loan early. Be sure to check for prepayment penalties in loan offers and consider how they may impact your ability to save money by paying off the loan ahead of schedule.

7. **Review the Repayment Schedule:** Understand the repayment schedule of each loan offer, including the frequency of payments and any grace periods. Make sure the repayment schedule aligns with your budget and financial goals.

8. **Compare Additional Features:** Some loan offers may come with additional features such as flexible repayment options, loan refinancing options, or the ability to defer payments under certain circumstances. Consider these features when comparing loan offers to find the best fit for your needs.

By following these steps and carefully comparing loan offers and interest rates, you can make an informed decision that aligns with your financial goals and helps you save money in the long run. Remember to read the terms and conditions of each loan offer carefully and seek clarification from the lender if you have any questions.

Avoiding Debt Traps When Making Major Purchases

Making major purchases can be exciting, but it's important to approach them with caution to avoid falling into debt traps. Here are some strategies to help you make smart choices and steer clear of financial pitfalls:

1. **Set a Realistic Budget:** Before making a major purchase, take the time to create a detailed budget that includes all of your expenses and income. Determine how much you can comfortably afford to spend on the item without jeopardizing your financial stability. Be honest with yourself about what you can realistically afford, and stick to your budget.
2. **Comparison Shop:** Don't rush into making a major purchase without doing your homework. Research different options, compare prices from various retailers, and look for deals or discounts that can help

you save money. By taking the time to shop around, you can make sure you're getting the best value for your money.

3. **Consider Financing Options Carefully:** If you need to finance a major purchase, such as a car or a home, it's important to explore your financing options carefully. Compare interest rates, loan terms, and fees from different lenders to find the most favorable deal. Avoid high-interest loans or credit cards with unfavorable terms that can lead to excessive debt.

4. **Save Up for a Down Payment:** Whenever possible, try to save up for a down payment before making a major purchase. By putting down a substantial amount of money upfront, you can reduce the amount you need to borrow and lower your monthly payments. Saving for a down payment also demonstrates financial responsibility and helps you avoid excessive debt.

5. **Avoid Impulse Buying:** It can be tempting to make a major purchase on a whim, especially if you see a flashy advertisement or a limited-time offer. However, impulse buying can lead to overspending and accumulating debt that you may struggle to

repay. Take the time to carefully consider your purchase and weigh the pros and cons before committing to a major expense.

6. **Plan for Unexpected Expenses:** When making a major purchase, it's important to factor in potential unexpected expenses, such as maintenance costs, repairs, or insurance premiums. By planning ahead and setting aside funds for these additional expenses, you can avoid financial stress and prevent debt from piling up.

By following these tips and being mindful of your financial decisions, you can avoid debt traps and maintain a healthy financial outlook when making major purchases. Remember to prioritize your long-term financial well-being and make informed choices that align with your goals and values.

Chapter 5:
Protecting Your Credit

Importance of Monitoring Your Credit Report:

Monitoring your credit report is a crucial aspect of managing your finances effectively and responsibly, especially as a teenager diving into the world of credit. Here are some key reasons why it is essential to regularly check and monitor your credit report:

1. **Detect Errors and Fraudulent Activity:** By reviewing your credit report regularly, you can spot any errors or inaccuracies that may be present. These errors could range from incorrect personal information to unauthorized accounts opened in your name due to identity theft or fraud. Detecting these issues early on can help you take prompt action to rectify them.

2. **Maintain Good Credit Standing:** Your credit report reflects your credit history, including factors like payment history, credit utilization, and credit accounts. By monitoring your credit report, you can

ensure that all your payments are being reported accurately and that there are no missed or late payments dragging down your credit score. A good credit standing is essential for future financial endeavors, such as obtaining loans or credit cards.

3. **Prevent Identity Theft:** Identity theft is a serious concern in today's digital age. By keeping an eye on your credit report, you can quickly identify any suspicious activity that may indicate someone has stolen your identity. This could include new accounts opened without your knowledge or unfamiliar inquiries into your credit history. Taking action promptly can help prevent further damage to your credit and finances.

4. **Track Your Progress:** Monitoring your credit report allows you to track your financial progress over time. You can see how your credit score fluctuates based on your financial decisions and behaviors. This insight can help you make adjustments to improve your credit score and overall financial health.

5. **Prepare for Future Financial Goals:** Whether you plan to apply for a student loan, a car loan, or a credit card in the future, having a good credit score is

crucial. By monitoring your credit report, you can ensure that your credit history is accurate and up-to-date, increasing your chances of approval for loans and credit at favorable terms.

In conclusion, monitoring your credit report is a proactive step towards managing your finances responsibly and safeguarding your financial future. By staying informed about your credit history and taking action to address any issues that arise, you can maintain good credit standing and make informed financial decisions as a teen and beyond.

How to Detect and Prevent Identity Theft

Detecting and preventing identity theft is crucial in today's digital world, where personal information can easily be compromised. This requires a combination of vigilance, proactive measures, and quick action if you suspect your identity has been compromised. Here are some steps you can take:

Detection:

1. **Monitor Financial Statements:** Regularly review your bank statements, credit card statements, and

any other financial accounts for unfamiliar transactions.

2. **Check Credit Reports:** Obtain and review your credit reports from major credit bureaus (Experian, Equifax, TransUnion) annually or use a credit monitoring service to keep track of changes.
3. **Monitor Credit Scores:** Monitor your credit scores for any sudden drops that could indicate fraudulent activity.
4. **Watch for Missing Mail:** If you stop receiving mail or bills, it could be a sign that someone has changed your mailing address.
5. **Review Medical Bills:** Check medical bills and insurance statements for services you didn't receive.
6. **Be Cautious of Unsolicited Communications:** Be wary of unexpected calls, emails, or messages requesting personal information.
7. **Review Social Media Privacy Settings:** Ensure your social media profiles are set to private, limiting the amount of personal information visible to the public.

Prevention:

1. **Strong Passwords:** Use strong, unique passwords for each online account, and consider using a password

manager to keep track of them.

2. **Secure Personal Information:** Shred documents containing sensitive information before disposing of them, and be cautious about sharing personal information online or over the phone.

3. **Use Two-Factor Authentication:** Enable two-factor authentication whenever possible to add an extra layer of security to your accounts.

4. **Update Security Software:** Keep your antivirus and anti-malware software up to date to protect against malicious software that could compromise your information.

5. **Secure Internet Connection:** Avoid using public Wi-Fi for sensitive transactions, as it can be more vulnerable to hackers.

6. **Be Cautious of Phishing Attempts:** Don't click on links or download attachments from unfamiliar or suspicious emails, as they could be phishing attempts.

7. **Freeze Credit:** Consider freezing your credit with the major credit bureaus to prevent new accounts from being opened in your name without your permission.

8. **Review Privacy Settings:** Regularly review and

update the privacy settings on your online accounts to control who can see your personal information.

9. **Protect Your Social Security Number:** Avoid carrying your Social Security card in your wallet, and be cautious about who you share your Social Security number with.

10. **Be Vigilant:** Stay alert for signs of identity theft and act quickly if you notice any suspicious activity.

If you suspect that you are a victim of identity theft, you should contact your financial institutions and credit bureaus immediately to report the issue and take steps to mitigate the damage. Additionally, you may consider filing a report with the Federal Trade Commission (FTC) and local law enforcement.

Steps to Take If You Become a Victim of Fraud

1. **Stay Calm:** The first and most important step to take if you become a victim of fraud is to stay calm. It can be a very stressful situation, but it is crucial to keep a clear head and take action promptly.

2. **Contact the Financial Institution:** If you notice any unauthorized transactions on your credit card or

bank account, contact the financial institution immediately. They can help you freeze your account to prevent further unauthorized transactions.

3. **Report the Fraud:** Contact the police and file a report about the fraud. Make sure to provide as much detail as possible, including any evidence you have of the fraudulent activity.

4. **Notify Credit Reporting Agencies:** If you suspect that your identity has been stolen, contact the major credit reporting agencies - Equifax, Experian, and TransUnion - to place a fraud alert on your credit report. This can help prevent further fraudulent activity using your personal information.

5. **Monitor Your Accounts:** Keep a close eye on your credit card and bank statements for any suspicious activity. Report any unauthorized transactions to the financial institution immediately.

6. **Change Your Passwords:** If you suspect that your online accounts have been compromised, change your passwords immediately. Use strong, unique passwords for each account to prevent further unauthorized access.

7. **Keep Detailed Records:** Keep a record of all

communication with the financial institution, police, and credit reporting agencies regarding the fraud. This can help you track the progress of the investigation and provide evidence if needed.
8. **Stay Informed:** Stay informed about the latest scams and fraud tactics to protect yourself from future incidents. Educate yourself about ways to prevent fraud and protect your personal information.

By following these steps, you can take control of the situation and minimize the impact of fraud on your finances and credit. Remember, it is important to act quickly and decisively if you become a victim of fraud.

Tips for Safeguarding Your Personal Information

In today's digital age, safeguarding your personal information is more important than ever. From online shopping to social media accounts, our personal data is constantly at risk of falling into the wrong hands. As a teen navigating the world of credit and finances, it's crucial to take steps to protect your sensitive information. Here are some tips to help you safeguard your personal data:

1. **Be Cautious with Sharing Information:** Avoid sharing personal details such as your full name, address, phone number, or social security number online unless it's absolutely necessary. Be vigilant about who you share your information with, especially on social media platforms.
2. **Use Strong Passwords:** Create strong and unique passwords for your online accounts. Avoid using easy-to-guess passwords like "123456" or "password." Instead, opt for a combination of letters, numbers, and symbols to enhance security.
3. **Secure Your Devices:** Keep your devices, including smartphones, tablets, and computers, secure by setting up passwords or passcodes. Enable features like fingerprint recognition or facial recognition to add an extra layer of security.
4. **Beware of Phishing Scams:** Be cautious of phishing scams, where fraudsters try to trick you into revealing personal information through fake emails or websites. Avoid clicking on suspicious links or providing sensitive details to unknown sources.
5. **Monitor Your Accounts:** Regularly monitor your bank accounts, credit card statements, and credit

reports for any unauthorized or suspicious activity. Report any discrepancies immediately to your financial institution.

6. **Shred Sensitive Documents:** When disposing of old documents containing personal information, such as bank statements or credit card offers, make sure to shred them to prevent identity theft.

7. **Secure Your Social Security Number:** Your social security number is a valuable piece of information that should be kept confidential. Avoid carrying your social security card with you and only provide it when absolutely necessary.

8. **Use Secure Networks:** When accessing sensitive information online, such as making online purchases or checking your bank account, use secure networks like your home Wi-Fi instead of public Wi-Fi networks, which are more vulnerable to hacking.

9. **Stay Informed:** Keep yourself informed about the latest cybersecurity threats and updates. Be proactive in learning about best practices for protecting your personal information online.

By following these tips and staying vigilant about protecting your personal information, you can reduce the risk of falling victim to identity theft or fraud. Remember, your personal data is valuable, so take the necessary steps to keep it safe and secure.

Chapter 6:
Credit for the Future

Planning for the Future with Credit in Mind

Planning for the future with credit in mind is crucial for teens as they begin to navigate the world of personal finance. Understanding how credit works and how to use it responsibly can set the foundation for a healthy financial future. Here are some key points to consider when planning for the future with credit in mind:

1. **Setting Financial Goals:** Before utilizing credit, it's important to establish clear financial goals. Whether it's saving for college, purchasing a car, or planning for a vacation, having specific goals in mind can help you make informed decisions about when and how to use credit.
2. **Building a Good Credit History:** Your credit history is a record of how you've managed credit and debt in the past. Building a good credit history early on can open up opportunities for better interest rates on

loans and credit cards in the future. Paying bills on time, keeping credit card balances low, and avoiding opening multiple accounts at once are all ways to establish and maintain a positive credit history.

3. **Understanding Credit Scores:** Your credit score is a numerical representation of your creditworthiness based on factors such as payment history, credit utilization, length of credit history, types of credit, and new credit accounts. Understanding how credit scores are calculated and knowing your own score can help you make smarter financial decisions and work towards improving your score over time.

4. **Creating a Budget:** Budgeting is a key component of managing credit responsibly. By tracking your income and expenses, you can ensure that you're living within your means and avoiding unnecessary debt. A budget can also help you prioritize your financial goals and make informed decisions about when to use credit for purchases.

5. **Using Credit Wisely:** When using credit, it's important to do so wisely and responsibly. Avoid maxing out credit cards, only charge what you can afford to pay off each month, and be mindful of

interest rates and fees. By using credit responsibly, you can avoid falling into debt and set yourself up for a more secure financial future.

6. **Planning for Emergencies:** Having a plan in place for unexpected expenses can help you avoid relying on credit in times of financial hardship. Building an emergency fund with three to six months' worth of living expenses can provide a safety net and reduce the need to turn to credit cards or loans when unexpected costs arise.

By taking a proactive approach to planning for the future with credit in mind, teens can set themselves up for financial success and build a strong foundation for a secure financial future. Learning how to use credit responsibly, understanding the importance of building a good credit history, and making informed decisions about when and how to use credit are all essential steps in navigating the world of personal finance as a teen.

Understanding the Long-Term Impact of Credit Decisions

Understanding the long-term impact of credit decisions is

crucial for teenagers as they begin their journey into the world of financial responsibility. By grasping the implications of their credit choices, teens can make informed decisions that will positively influence their financial future.

One key aspect to consider is the concept of credit scores. A credit score is a numerical representation of an individual's creditworthiness based on factors such as payment history, amounts owed, length of credit history, new credit, and types of credit used. Every financial decision that involves credit, such as taking out a loan or using a credit card, can impact a person's credit score. It is important for teens to understand that a good credit score can open up opportunities for favorable interest rates on loans and credit cards and even impact their ability to rent an apartment or secure a job in the future.

Furthermore, teens must recognize the potential long-term consequences of accumulating debt. While it may be tempting to make purchases with borrowed money, it is crucial to understand that debt comes with interest charges that can accumulate over time. Failing to make timely payments on credit accounts can lead to late fees, higher interest rates, and a negative impact on credit scores. This, in turn, can make it more difficult to secure loans or credit in the future and can even limit opportunities for financial growth and stability.

Teens should also be aware of the importance of responsible financial habits in shaping their long-term financial well-being. By making wise credit decisions, such as paying bills on time, avoiding unnecessary debt, and keeping credit card balances low, teenagers can set themselves up for a solid financial foundation as they transition into adulthood.

In conclusion, understanding the long-term impact of credit decisions is essential for teenagers to build a secure financial future. By being informed and proactive in managing their credit, teens can avoid common pitfalls and set themselves up for success in their financial lives.

Setting Financial Goals and Using Credit Wisely to Achieve Them

Setting financial goals and using credit wisely to achieve them are crucial steps in managing your money effectively. This section is designed to help teenagers understand the importance of setting financial goals and using credit responsibly to reach those goals.

Setting financial goals is the first step in taking control of your financial future. Whether your goal is to save up for a car, go to college, start a business, or buy a house, having a clear goal in mind can help you stay focused and motivated. When setting financial goals, it's important to make them specific, measurable, achievable, relevant, and time-bound (SMART). This means setting a clear target amount, breaking it down into smaller milestones, and setting a deadline for achieving each milestone.

Once you have set your financial goals, the next step is to create a plan to achieve them. This plan should include a budget that outlines your income, expenses, and savings goals. It's essential to prioritize your goals and allocate your resources accordingly. This is where credit can come into play as a useful tool to help you achieve your goals faster. However, it's important to use credit wisely to avoid falling into debt traps.

Using credit wisely means only borrowing what you can afford to repay and making timely payments to avoid high interest charges and late fees. It's crucial to understand how credit works, including interest rates, credit scores, and the impact of borrowing on your financial future. When using credit to achieve your financial goals, it's essential to compare different credit options, shop around for the best rates, and read the terms and conditions carefully to avoid any surprises.

In summary, setting financial goals and using credit wisely go hand in hand in helping you achieve financial success. By setting clear goals, creating a plan, and using credit responsibly, you can take control of your finances, build a strong financial foundation, and work towards achieving your dreams.

Tips for Maintaining Good Credit Throughout Your Life

1. **Pay your bills on time:** Timely payment of bills is crucial for maintaining a good credit score. Late payments can negatively impact your credit history, so make sure to pay your bills by the due date each month.
2. **Keep credit card balances low:** High credit card balances relative to your credit limit can hurt your credit score. Aim to keep your credit card balances

low and pay off your balances in full each month whenever possible.

3. **Monitor your credit report regularly:** It's important to regularly review your credit report to check for any errors or fraudulent activity. By monitoring your credit report, you can address any issues promptly and ensure that your credit information is accurate.

4. **Avoid opening too many new accounts:** Opening multiple new credit accounts within a short period can lower your credit score. Be selective about applying for new credit and only open accounts that you truly need.

5. **Maintain a mix of credit types:** Having a diverse mix of credit types, such as credit cards, installment loans, and a mortgage, can demonstrate responsible credit management. Aim to maintain a healthy mix of credit accounts to show lenders that you can handle different types of credit responsibly.

6. **Don't close old accounts:** Closing old credit accounts can shorten your credit history and potentially lower your credit score. Instead of closing old accounts, consider keeping them open and using them occasionally to maintain a positive credit history.

7. **Communicate with creditors:** If you're experiencing financial difficulties that may impact your ability to make payments on time, it's important to communicate with your creditors. Many creditors are willing to work with you to establish a payment plan or modify your terms to help you manage your debt effectively.

By following these tips and practicing responsible credit management habits, you can maintain good credit throughout your life and build a solid financial foundation for the future.

Conclusion

Congratulations! You've reached the end of "Dollars and Sense: A Teen's Guide to Credit." Throughout this book, we've covered a wide range of topics designed to equip you with the knowledge and skills necessary to navigate the world of credit responsibly. From understanding the basics of credit to managing credit cards, using credit for major purchases, protecting your credit, and planning for the future, you now have a solid foundation to build upon as you journey toward financial independence.

In the fast-paced world we live in, where financial decisions can have long-lasting consequences, it's crucial for young adults like yourself to be informed and empowered. By mastering the principles outlined in this book, you've taken an important step toward securing a stable financial future.

Remember, credit is a tool that, when used wisely, can open doors and provide opportunities for growth and financial freedom. However, it's essential to approach credit with caution and responsibility. Always strive to make informed decisions, prioritize financial literacy, and practice good money management habits.

As you continue on your financial journey, keep in mind the importance of ongoing learning and adaptation. The world of credit is constantly evolving, and staying informed about new developments and best practices will serve you well in the years to come.

Finally, never underestimate the power of setting and working towards your financial goals. Whether it's saving for a dream vacation, purchasing your first car, or investing in your education, having clear objectives can help guide your financial decisions and keep you on track toward success.

Thank you for joining me on this journey through the world of credit. I hope that the insights and strategies shared in this book will serve you well as you navigate the exciting road ahead. Here's to a future filled with financial confidence, security, and prosperity!

Best wishes, Mandy Oglethorpe

www.ingramcontent.com/pod-product-compliance
Lightning Source LLC
Chambersburg PA
CBHW030047230526
45471CB00003B/982